Paws for Purrtection:

200 Haikus Celebrating the Power of Dogs and Cats

Tarun Reddy

Paws for Purrfection

Editing by Ruth Zurawka

Formatting by dMon Publishing, LLC
www.dmonpublishing.com

Front cover photo provided by iStockphoto.com
©mashabuba

Paperback ISBN-10: 0615925391
Paperback ISBN-13: 978-0615925394

First Edition

DEDICATION

This book is dedicated to anyone whose life is made brighter on a daily basis by the love (or mischief) of a dog or cat.

ACKNOWLEDGMENTS

When writing a book, the process goes far beyond the trials and tribulations experienced by the author. That is certainly this case with this book. Ruth Zurawka, an animal lover, high school classmate, computer programmer, parachutist, scooter owner (oh my is there anything she doesn't do?) provided editorial assistance on a scale that is really difficult to quantify.

Ruth, an avid fan of cats and mice, took a critical eye to "Paws" by looking at each haiku individually and then going back through the book to see if any themes were repeated. She also spent a significant amount of time double-checking the facts at the bottom of each page to ensure accuracy and clarity. When writing a book with so much information, it is easy for an author, such as myself, to suffer a literary form of tunnel vision.

I also want to thank the following people for lending their support during the writing process. In some cases, the stories I heard about their pets served as inspiration for a haiku. Among those I need to thank are: Alex and Sarah Brewsaugh, Jill Gardner, Lisa Ford, Joy Robinson, Sharon Sumner Lott, Larry and Stacy Wheeler, Lorena Anderson and John and Kristyn McCrohan. It would also be remiss if I forgot to mention Christina Shakus. Her use of social media to talk about current pets and early departed ones always amazes me and served as an ongoing inspiration during the writing process.

As you see in the introduction, these friends were critical to generating ideas in my head, not only for the haikus, but also the "Something to Get Your Paws On" sections. In many cases, I would see information they had posted and it would make me curious. So I would do some web-based research to see if I could come up with an interesting factoid.

As always, I am grateful for my parents and my sister Neena. Their support and constructive criticism are an integral part of my writing career. Finally, I must mention my son Akhil, who had to deal with me mumbling in haiku during the writing of this book.

Introduction

I have always been amazed at the bond that people have with their dogs and cats because, in many cases, it seems like that connection is as strong as a human relationship. The strength that pet owners get from their furry friends amazes me because dogs and cats do not speak English. People shower upon them a level of affection that is worthy of a Shakespearean play.

While I have never owned a cat or a dog, the way my friends interact and speak of their dogs and cats has left an indelible mark on me. To hear a friend ask their beagle if it's too cold in the house or wonder aloud if their cat is lonely during the weekday makes me chuckle. At the same time, though, I understand that deep bond people develop with pets, especially if they had pets during their childhood.

After I released my first book, the best seller "Brew-ku: Where Coffee Intersects with Life," I was thinking of other topics that might be appropriate for the basis of a book of poetry. When I found out how many people in the United States own cats and dogs, I knew that this would be a great idea for my follow-up book.

What's that? How many people own dogs and cats in the United States?   Rather than me telling you the answer right now, I'll let you find out by reading the book! On each of the following pages, there is haiku with a fun fact or statistic about dogs and cats. I have always been fascinated with trivia and thought it would be fun to include canine and feline trivia in the book.

Unlike "Brew-ku," I did not translate the haikus into Japanese because of technical issues associated with trying to convert a paperback into an eBook. Plus, most of the poems have specific English names for the pets and I figured it would be awkward to have English interspersed among the Japanese characters.

Rather than dividing the book into two distinct sections—one with dog haikus and the other one with haikus about felines, I decided to make things a little more interesting by have two poems about dogs followed by two poems about cats throughout the book. This way, it would force dog and cat owners to read the entire book, rather than just reading one section about dogs.

You'll also notice that I repeat names for the dogs and cats referenced in the poems. Part of me did this as a way to recognize friends across the county who share a special bond with their pets. But there was also another, far more practical reason for taking this approach. I figured it would be more interesting to see a name such as "Nala" and "Chester" in print, rather than having to say "dog" or "cat" on each page. Plus, having specific names in the haikus made it easier for me to follow the 5-7-5 syllable structure by giving me a character on which I could base each poem.

Compiling the various facts, statistics and anecdotes for the "Something to Get Your Paws On" section proved to be more challenging thancomposing the "Something to Sip On" section in Brew-ku. I say that because there were many instances with this book where I would assume that I had an original fact or statistic on a page, only to have Ruth politely mention "You already mentioned this fact on page 32." Ah, editors, I do not know where I would be without them.

I don't own a dog

Nor fancy purebred feline

I'm just a writer

Something to get your paws on: There are approximately 86.4 million cats in the U.S., according to the Humane Society of the United States.

A burst of sunrise

Neighbor with dachshund stops by

My lawn, fertilized

Something to get your paws on: Dog owners spent an average of $43 on toys for their canines in 2012, according to the American Pet Products Association.

Return from work trip,

Expecting a happy cat;

How dare you leave me!

Something to get your paws on: The Akita is a Japanese breed. Many people in Japan believe that having an Akita at home brings good luck and prosperity. Helen Keller brought the first Akita to the United States in 1937.

My black wool sweater

Adorned with hair from white cat

Unwanted add-on

Something to get your paws on: Basset hounds are one of six recognized basset breeds in France. They were originally bred to hunt rabbits and hares.

All you need is love

And a warm furry feline

Stealing your blanket

Something to get your paws on: The American Bobtail cat originated in the Southwestern United States in the 1960s.

More than just a pet

Sharing our lives, joy, sadness

Pets are family

Something to get your paws on: The Belgian Malinois is a shepherd dog that gets its name from the Belgian city of Malines. The dogs are popular among police departments for detecting explosives and narcotics.

It's not yet sunrise

But Holly is in a rush

To go walk outside

Something to get your paws on: Balinese cats are related to Siamese cats. They tend to have minimal shedding and softer coats compared to other cats.

A warm fire soothes

Chester rests across her lap

Quiet, TV on

Something to get your paws on: The Chinese Shar Pei was once one of the rarest dogs in the world. It has a bluish tongue and deep, dark wrinkles. The breed originated in Korea and the name is a variation of "sa peih," which means "sand skin" in Cantonese. The dogs were extremely rare. In fact, the American Kennel Club did not recognize the breed until 1991.

Running up to me

Pointing towards the kitchen

Water bowl empty

Something to get your paws on: Breeders in England created the Bullmastiff in the nineteenth century to help pull buses that had broken down. The heritage is a combination of the English bulldog and Old English Mastiff.

Barking! Not sure why

Chandler stares out the window

Passing cars excite

Something to get your paws on: The Chihuahua has an interesting history because there is no definitive explanation for how they came to be. One possible explanation is that they descended from the Techichi breed, which was popular with the Toltec tribe.

Under the sofa

Forty tennis balls appear

So that's where they went!

Something to get your paws on: Greyhounds exert so much energy during a race that many lose up to five pounds during a competition.

As I read comics

Nala hisses. Wonder why

She dislikes Garfield

Something to get your paws on: The Manx cat, which originated on the Isle of Man, does not have a tail. Some people believe the cats came from the Spanish Armada.

Scratching! Won't be still!

Jodi escapes my tight grasp

Trying to cut nails

Something to get your paws on: The Munchkin cat breed originated in Louisiana. In 1983, Sandra Hochenedel found two pregnant cats. She kept one and gave away the other. Hochenedel's cat gave birth to kittens that were short-legged.

So many choices

I see, wet and dry cat food

Need time to decide

Something to get your paws on: There are two types of corgis, the "Cardigan" and the "Pembroke." Both breeds started appearing in dog shows around 1925. Queen Elizabeth owns 16 Corgis.

Dog park gets crowded

On Saturdays -- a great way

To meet new women

Something to get your paws on: Doberman Pinschers have been around since the nineteenth century and were previously used as police or guard dogs. They are named after German dog breeder Karl Friederich Louis Dobermann.

My sweet pit bull Hal

Scares other dog owners but

He's a sweetie pie

Something to get your paws on: California Spangled cats look wild but are actually domestic felines. They are a crossbreed of many cats including the American and British short hair cats.

A frisbee gets tossed

Fiona stares, doesn't move

I go to fetch it

Something to get your paws on: The Devon Rex is a cat with very soft curly hair that is similar to the Cornish Rex. Devon Rexes were first spotted near a tin mine near the British city of Buckfastleigh in Devon, England.

A four -hour nap

Sam is now wide awake but

Wonders about food

Something to get your paws on: The German Spitz Mittel is the third largest dog within the Spitz breed. In Germany, a Spitz that is not a solid color may not be entered into a dog show as an authentic Spitz.

As I pace worried

Hunter is close behind me

Puts my mind at ease

Something to get your paws on: The American Kennel Club was formed in 1884 in New York City. The group recognizes 150 breeds of dogs. There are 600 individual clubs within the organization.

Shane is selective

About the steak bones he likes

Premium ones, please

Something to get your paws on: The Federation Cynologique Internationale (FCI) includes 86 member nations. The AKC is not part of FCI, which is based in Thuin, Belgium.

A long car journey

She's content to stare outside

The miles roll by

Something to get your paws on: The Burmese (Myanmar) cat became popular in the United States in the 1930s. Joseph Thompson, a retired navy psychiatrist, is credited with developing the true breed.

Quiet time at beach

Walking along the white sands

With curious dog

Something to get your paws on: The word "tabby" evolved from British, French and Arabic words. The British used the term "taffeta."

As lunch guests arrive

Hal is nowhere to be found

Hide until they leave

Something to get your paws on: The Hungarian Wirehaired Vizsla is known as a good hunting dog. The plural of viszla is "viszlas" in English but is "vizlak" in Hungarian. Their coats are wiry, close lying, dense and strong.

My dog keeps barking

While Kayla practices flute;

Odd background music

Something to get your paws on: Dalmatians get their name from the Croatian region known as Dalmatia. Dalmatia also refers to clothing worn by priests and deacons.

Nala scratches ears

Can't find any fleas on her

A vet trip needed

Something to get your paws on: Jim Davis, the creator of the popular cartoon "Garfield," named the character after his grandfather, James A. Garfield Davis.

A freshly made bed

Becomes totally messy

Housework! What's the use?

Something to get your paws on: The superstition that claims it is bad luck if a black cat crosses your path may have originated during the Middle Ages. During that time, people believed black cats were witches in disguise.

Tarun Reddy

I'm reading in bed

With the lights on, but Scooter

Wants them switched off, now

Something to get your paws on: The Caucasian shepherd is one of the most popular dog breeds in Russia. These dogs are popular because they have a reputation for protecting flocks of sheep. Caucasian shepherds can be found in nations such as Armenia, Georgia and Azerbaijan.

Scooter runs quickly

Finds refuge under table

A car backfires

Something to get your paws on: Labradors are very athletic dogs and love to swim. They originated on St. John Island, which is part of the Canadian province of Newfoundland. Labs are the result of a cross breeding between Mastiffs and St. John dogs.

Scamper sniffs slowly

Eying my chocolate bar

No! It's poisonous!

Something to get your paws on: Pietro Della Valle mentioned the existence of Persian cats in his book "Trip to Turkey, Persia and India in 54 Letters." He saw the cats in the Iranian city of Isfahan in the 1620s.

Nala grabs pillows

Pretending to hide in them

A good morning laugh

Something to get your paws on: The Maneki Neko, or "beckoning cat," is a Japanese calico cat that is associated with good luck. Many Japanese keep maneki neko figurines in their house.

Tarun Reddy

Sarah sees my mug

A smiling cat logo

She squints, runs away

Something to get your paws on: Francis Galton invented the dog whistle in 1876. A human's hearing range is between 20 hertz and 20 kilohertz (KHz). By comparison, a dog's hearing range is around 40 Hz to 60 kHz while the Cat's is (55 Hz up to 79 kHz).

Working on new slides

Thumper barks at each new frame

Canine editor

Something to get your paws on: Edward Lowe invented kitty litter in 1947. Lowe got the idea for kitty litter after a neighbor asked him to create something that was more effective than ashes, which were commonly used to neutralize cat odor.

Running late for work

Can't find my new eyeglasses

Silly cat hid them

Something to get your paws on: The Lhasa Apso originated in Tibet. Monks used the dogs to provide interior security at temples. Lhasa is the capital city of Tibet and "apso" means "bearded" in the Tibetan language.

Nala, so ticklish

I touch her paws and belly

She really loves that

Something to get your paws on: The Nova Scotia Duck Tolling retriever is often referred to as a Toller. The art of enticing waterfowl to come close to hunters is known as "tolling."

Worried about cat

Falling off the stair railing

Double-sided tape

Something to get your paws on: The "curl" in the American Curl cat refers to the shape of its ears. The curling is considered a genetic trait and not a deformity.

In family room

Packing material mess

Tom had fun last night!

Something to get your paws on: The Savannah cat is a hybrid that resulted from mating a Bengal cat with a Serval cat. These cats tend to be larger than other cats and often weigh around thirty five pounds.

Late night, my beagle

Starts barking, but nothing's there

Attention seeker

Something to get your paws on: When the Titanic sunk on April 14, 1912, three dogs survived: a Pomeranian, a Pekinese and a Newfoundland.

I'm watching football

Chester steals the remote, now

We're watching Lifetime

Something to get your paws on: There are about 78,000 pet hotels in the United States according to market research firm, Ibis. These businesses employed 127,000 people and generated revenue of $5 billion in 2011.

Great day at the park

Amber jumping through three hoops

She'll sleep well tonight

Something to get your paws on: Dog biscuits may have originated in a London butcher shop. Some people say a butcher in the 1800s was trying to add more food items to his store's selection and tried baking biscuits. But when the butcher tried the biscuits, they were terrible. He gave one to his dog who loved it.

A tuna sandwich

On my plate; Ish wants a bite

But I won't let him

Something to get your paws on: There are four categories of tails for Cymric cats: rumpy, longy, rumpy riser and stumpy. Rumpies do not have tails, which means they cannot compete in shows.

Can't find Emily!

Looking here and there! Panic!

Laughing from rafters

Something to get your paws on: There are more than 500 million domestic cats around the world. The United States has the most cats while China comes in second with 53.4 million felines.

At the pool party

Tempo watches and barks when

She sees belly flops

Something to get your paws on: The scientific name for the plant that contains catnip is Nepeta cataria. It is also sometimes called catmint or catswort.

I'm taking a nap

Pepper brings me a gross gift

A freshly killed mouse

Something to get your paws on: A cat's claws have layers of skin similar to an onion. Normally, the claws will shed. The outer layer of claw tissue is continually growing and must be trimmed.

Friend knits a sweater

For my sweet dachshund, Diva

She is not impressed

Something to get your paws on: Cats are super fecund, which means kittens in one litter may have different fathers.

Old carpet removed

Rolled up in corner, Della

Is surfing on it

Something to get your paws on: The Association for Pet Obesity Prevention said in a 2012 study that 55% of cats are overweight or obese.

Twirling basketball

On my finger, my tabby

Eyes are fixated

Something to get your paws on: One in seven dogs has skin allergies, according to a study from Veterinary Pet Insurance.

I'm watching Macy's

Turkey Day Parade, Snoopy

Float makes Diva bark!

Something to get your paws on: President Theodore Roosevelt was quite fond of the Catahoula Leopard Dog, especially for hunting. The canine gets its name from Catahoula Parish in Louisiana, where the breed originated.

Neighbor's terrier

Barking loudly can be heard

Over lawn mowing

Something to get your paws on: Farmers along the border between Scotland and England developed the border collie breed to help with the herding of sheep.

Neighbor with poodles

Stops at my lawn, gives advice

Listen, and ignore

Something to get your paws on: Cats usually have 38 chromosomes, but there are some breeds with 36 or 37 chromosomes.

Special gift for Ish

To keep busy during day

A new scratching post

Something to get your paws on: The Chartreux cat is of French origin. French monks in the city of Grenoble (about five hours south of Paris) created the Chartreux. The monks wanted cats to catch mice in order to protect their food supply.

Booboo runs to me

Runs away just as quickly

Can't catch silly tail

Something to get your paws on: Hip dysplasia is the most common form of arthritis in dogs. It is often caused by a femur that has an irregular fit with the pelvic socket. Genetic history is the greatest indicator of a dog's likelihood of developing this disease.

Scratching Nala's ear

Creates a gentle purring

As sunset takes hold

Something to get your paws on: In January 2011, it was reported that a border collie named Chaser had learned 1,022 words and had a distinct response to each word. John Pilley and Allison Reed, psychologists at Wofford College, taught Chaser as many words as the average three-year old toddler knows.

Tarun Reddy

Knitting a sweater;

It's not for me, it's for my

Charming brown spaniel

Something to get your paws on: Many ancient Egyptians considered cats to be more important than humans. There was a deity known as Mafdet, which may have been the first religious deity associated with cats. Egyptian folklore states that Mafdet once killed a snake with her paws.

Tomba in kitchen

As I prepare chicken stock

He's eyeing the bones

Something to get your paws on: The top ten most common cat names in the U.S. in 2012 were: Kitty, Tiger, Bella, Kitten, Smokey, Max, Tigger, Shadow, Chloe, and Lucy.

Watching kids' soccer

Tomba barks when the goalie

Blocks a quick, hard shot

Something to get your paws on: Beagles are a member of the hound group. They were originally developed as scent hounds for tracking hare, rabbits and other small animals. Their keen sense of smell has also allowed law enforcement agencies to use them for tracking illegal imports of agriculture.

Panda barks loudly,

As we walk by the river;

She remembers well

Something to get your paws on: The Schnauzer originated in Germany in the fifteenth or sixteenth century. The dog gets its name from the German word "schnauze," which means "snout" in English.

Searching for my keys

I'm running from room to room

Panda stares and barks

Something to get your paws on: Animal historians believe that cats have been eating fish for more than 1,000 years because of the taste. In addition, fish are an excellent source of protein for the carnivorous feline.

Hanging Christmas lights,

Tomba doesn't notice them,

Until they're turned on

Something to get your paws on: Poodles originated in Germany and were known as "Pudlehounds." The word "pudel" means "to splash about" and "hund" means "dog" in German. There are three sizes of poodles: miniature, toy and standard.

Colt having much fun

Stomping on fresh bubble wrap

Popping sounds abound

Something to get your paws on: There are 43 teams in the National Collegiate Athletic Association that have the nickname "bulldogs." The first school on the list is Adrian College, while the last name on the list is Yale University.

Dog training session

Colt ignores trainer's commands

Patience required

Something to get your paws on: There are 21 schools with the nickname "wildcats" in the NCAA. The first team on this list is Abilene Christian University and the last school is Weber State University.

Tossing a baseball,

Booboo runs between friend, me

Cat in the middle

Something to get your paws on: The Turkish Van is one of the more unusual cat breeds in the world. The cats, which originated in Lake Van in Armenia, are known to enjoy swimming.

Nala so enjoys

The cord for my new cell phone

Must replace the cord

Something to get your paws on: The Ibizan hound resembles a deer because of its amber eyes, long ears and red and white fur. Ibiza is an island 50 miles from the coast of Valencia, Spain.

Tarun Reddy

Mobile apps for cats

Chasing five digital mice

Keeps them occupied

Something to get your paws on: Whippets are generally considered to be indoor dogs because of their quiet demeanor.

Web meeting started;

My cat runs into room, stares

Causing group laughter

Something to get your paws on: There is no such breed as a Cheshire cat. The term "Cheshire" refers to cats from Cheshire, England, who loved the abundance of milk and cream from the area's dairy farms.

My silly coon cats

Get excited by sounds of

A baby rattle

Something to get your paws on: In Greek mythology, people were often turned into cats. In some cases, this was because a god needed an animal to represent him. In other cases, being turned into a cat was considered punishment.

I'm brushing my teeth

Booboo watches the water

Thoroughly amused

Something to get your paws on: William Shakespeare used the phrase "Dogs of War" in Act Three, Scene One of "Julius Caesar." Shakespeare used the term to refer to soldiers. In modern times, "Dogs of War" refers to mercenaries.

Tarun Reddy

Singing to my cat

"Billie Jean," but sadly she's

Not a Michael fan

Something to get your paws on: It is estimated there are 300,000 feral cats roaming the streets of Rome. This population is divided into roughly 200 colonies. Women who feed these cats are known as "gattare" or volunteer cat caretakers.

Tomba playing with

A hairclip. So I snap it!

Rolls over in joy

Something to get your paws on: Scientists have estimated that a cat's sense of smell is fourteen times greater than a human's. That is because cats have twice as many receptors in their noses.

I'm trying to nap,

Constant noise from scratching post,

Keeping me awake

Something to get your paws on: The Pharaoh dog is both a family dog and hunting canine. When these dogs get excited, their noses and ears turn slightly red.

In the world of cats,

No fancy parks required;

Cat memes rule the day

Something to get your paws on: Dr. Clyde Keller created the Himalayan cat breed while working at Harvard University and the Virginia Cobb of Newton cattery. He started breeding Persian Cats with Siamese cats, creating a feline known as Newton's Debutante.

I'm ready to sleep,

My collie wants to go out;

And the collie wins

Something to get your paws on: Canadian Eskimo dogs have a fondness for cold weather and prefer sleeping outside.

Boyfriend allergic

To my precious Nala, so

Must find new boyfriend

Something to get your paws on: The Estrela Mountain Dog is native to Portugal and is used by farmers to guard their herds. Because of the region's isolated location, there is virtually no breeding with non-native canines.

Ivy at laptop,

Checking my email folder,

Four-legged blackmail

Something to get your paws on: Starting in the 1890s, breeders in Britain tried to create an all-brown cat. It wasn't until the 1950s that they succeeded by cross breeding a Siamese cat with a black short-hair cat. At first, these cats were known as Chestnut Brown Foreigns before the name was changed to the Havana Brown cat.

Champ loves Journey tunes

In the mornings he dances;

Don't stop retrievin'

Something to get your paws on: In the movie *Cinderella*, the name of the stepmother's cat was Lucifer. At one point in the movie, Cinderella gets mad at Lucifer and orders him to go outside.

Penny loves chewing

On plastic bags so I keep

Them away from her

Something to get your paws on: The Czech Wolf Dog has characteristics similar to German Shepherds and wolves. This breed typically reaches maturity by the age of three.

My tabby Nico,

She's being way too quiet

She's up to no good!

Something to get your paws on: The Finnish Spitz is known for hunting birds and small animals. They are typically 17 to 20 inches tall and weigh between 31 and 36 pounds.

Nico next to Champ

Both gems snoring quietly

Picture purrfect sight

Something to get your paws on: The term "calico" does not refer to a specific breed of cat. Instead, it refers to cats with a combination of black, red and white in their coats. Some cats with diluted amounts of gray, cream or white may also be known as calicos.

Hard to make cookies,

When my tabby falls asleep

On the cookie sheet

Something to get your paws on: There's a Welsh superstition that says whenever a cat's pupil broadens, rain is on the way.

Smoke detector beeps

My cat scurries to my bed,

Hiding from the noise

Something to get your paws on: People living in the Swiss Alps originally used St. Bernards to be rescue dogs rather than work dogs. The dogs can weigh between 140 and 270 pounds. The dogs get their name from St. Bernard Pass in Switzerland.

Tomba having fun

But runs away from loud sound

Of pressure cooker

Something to get your paws on: Most cats do not like to admit being ill and will often hide during a time of sickness.

Building furniture,

But Nala loves rolling wheels;

Assembly halted

Something to get your paws on: The Xoloitzcuintli is also known as the Mexican Hairless Dog and researchers believe the canine dates back to the Aztecs. Some people also use the nickname "Xolo" for the dog.

Folding bows for gifts,

Trying to keep them in row,

Asha disrupts row

Something to get your paws on: The Carolina Dog or "American Dingo" is believed to be the oldest dog species in North America. Images of the dogs have appeared on Native American rock paintings.

Nala excited

About her new set of wheels,

A swank pet stroller

Something to get your paws on: The Greek Harehound is a rare breed of scent hound that is only found in Southern Greece. The canines, which farmers use to hunt hares, have distinctive coats that are black and tan.

I'm washing dishes,

Ivy hops onto counter,

For a better view

Something to get your paws on: In Greek mythology, the goddess Hecate assumed the form of a cat in order to escape a monster known as Typhon. Afterward, she extended special treatment to all cats.

My parakeet chirps;

Champ moving toward his cage,

And the chirping stops

Something to get your paws on: More than 200 cats participated in an international beauty contest, which was held in Bucharest, Romania in 2013.

I need extra sleep;

Penny doesn't understand;

Door scratching persists

Something to get your paws on: Great Danes originated in Germany and were bred for hunting and to serve as guardians. The tallest Great Dane in the world, Zeus, is forty-four inches tall. He lives in Otsego, Michigan.

Tarun Reddy

Sipping coffee and

A roaring fire warms me,

Chester at my feet

Something to get your paws on: The British playwright
Ben Jonson used the phrase, "Curiosity Killed the Cat,"
in his 1598 play, "Every Man in His Humour." James
Allan Mair referred to the proverb in his 1873 book, "A
Handbook of Proverbs: English, Scottish, Irish,
American, Shakespearean and Scriptural and Family
Mottoes."

Purring so softly

But she's not really awake

Nala in dream state

Something to get your paws on: An Irish superstition claimed that if a canine howled near the house of a sick person, that meant there was no hope for the individual's recovery.

Be careful with cakes

Dogs and chocolate don't mix

Dangerous outcomes

Something to get your paws on: Most people who have pet allergies are allergic to pet dander rather than pet hair. Pet dander is similar to human dandruff although dander scales are much smaller.

Somewhere a feline

Is rolling her eyes, saying

Servant! Feed me now!

Something to get your paws on: While there aren't exact statistics available, it is estimated that between three million and four million dogs and cats are euthanized every year because of overpopulation.

River rushes by;

I wait for catfish to bite

Champ quietly sits

Something to get your paws on: A March 2011 study from Michigan State University found that people who walked their dogs exercised an hour a week more than dog owners who didn't walk their pets.

Buster and Chloe are

Chasing each other. I laugh

At this game of tag

Something to get your paws on: Heartworm, a condition caused by infected mosquitoes, is a growing problem in cats, although it is more prevalent in dogs. Heartworm causes lung disease in felines. A persistent cough, breathing problems and depression are often symptoms of heartworm.

At mirror, check hair

Squinting to see more clearly

Chester barks support

Something to get your paws on: Salukis, which originated in Egypt, are one of the world's oldest known dog breeds. Images of the dogs appear on tombs dating back to 2134 BC.

It's tough to impress

A chatty brunette when your

Collie won't stay still

Something to get your paws on: Southern Illinois University in Carbondale uses the nickname "salukis" for its sports teams. The university chose that nickname in part because the area around Carbondale is known as Little Egypt.

My hot date arrives

Colby hisses, then departs

Could be a bad sign

Something to get your paws on: A survey in 2010 found that 63% of dog owners and 58% of cat owners give their pets presents during Christmas. Americans spend about five billion dollars annually on gifts for cats and dogs.

My new puppy looks

Like a gorgeous St. Bernard

But he's a spaniel

Something to get your paws on: Pugs originated in China but became popular in Europe, especially in the Netherlands and England. The House of Stuart in England and the House of Orange in the Netherlands were especially fond of pugs. Medical research shows that pugs suffer from numerous ailments, including obesity, overeating and pharyngeal reflux

The fire crackles,

Henry turns, pants a little

Then stares at window

Something to get your paws on: Cat owners spent about four billion dollars on cat food in 2011 according to the American Pet Products Manufacturers Association. To put that number into perspective, Americans spend about three billion dollars annually on baby food.

Traffic light still red

Restless Henry wants to cross

Tug on leash, he's calm

Something to get your paws on: One-third of U.S. households own at least one cat, according to statistics from the Humane Society of the United States. In addition, 52% of cat owners have multiple felines.

Labrador's nose bleeds

Owner fearing the worst news

Nasal cancer threat

Something to get your paws on: As the name suggests, the Otterhound is a British breed that was created to hunt otters. There are fewer than a thousand of the animals alive. The Kennel Club (similar to the American Kennel Club in the United States) has named the Otterhound a vulnerable native breed.

Jogging with Henry

Makes me jealous. He's in great

Shape, but I struggle

Something to get your paws on: The Maltese is a dog that originated on the Isle of Malta and is sometimes referred to as the "Roman ladies dog." These dogs may also be known as "bichons," which comes from the French verb "bichonner" and means "to pamper."

My cat relishes

A nice massage whenever

It's cold in the house

Something to get your paws on: The Komondor is a popular dog for sheepherding or managing livestock. The dogs originated in Tibet with the Cumans. The Cumans fled Mongol invaders and eventually settled in Hungary.

While vacuuming,

Ivy stares at the patterns

Avoids walking there

Something to get your paws on: There are around 12 million feral cats in Australia. Research has shown these cats eat 186 species of native birds and 87 species of reptiles.

Back from a long walk,

Champ rushes to water bowl,

Needing to cool down

Something to get your paws on: About 35 percent of Canadian households own a cat, according to several studies. By comparison, about 32 percent of Canadians own at least one dog.

Music blasting, I

Struggle with Pilates moves;

Henry mocks me. Barks!

Something to get your paws on: The Japanese chin is also known as the Japanese spaniel. Some people say the dogs originated in 732 A.D. and came from China. Other historians say the dogs were from Korea. Prior to the chin's arrival, dogs in Japan were considered work animals. By contrast, chins were considered pets for enjoyment.

Rehearse for meeting

Using a laser pointer

Cat ballet begins

Something to get your paws on: The Greater Swiss Mountain dog is native to the Swiss Alps. The dogs are also known as Sennenhounds. "Sennen" is German and refers to the dairymen and farmers in the region. The dogs evolved based on the breeding of native Swiss canines with imported mastiffs.

I'm teasing Ivy

Placing a baseball cap on

Her cold furry head

Something to get your paws on: Cats are the only mammals that lack the ability to taste sweet things. Part of the reason for this is that cats lack a specific set of amino acids that enable sweet-related taste buds to work properly.

Sweeping the kitchen,

Hayden hides under the sink

A wise dog, indeed

Something to get your paws on: Breeders created the Chausie cat by mating a jungle cat with a domestic cat. The Latin name for a jungle cat is "Felis Chausis." The wild jungle cat typically lives along the Nile River.

Learning guitar chords

My chocolate lab suffers

As I play louder

Something to get your paws on: It takes between four and six months to train a hearing dog. The training includes: temperament evaluation, obedience training, socialization training and sound training.

Henry places paws

In my new, black running shoes

He should run for me

Something to get your paws on: Most police departments import dogs from Europe for training. These canines have typically trained in sports such as Schutzhund or French Ring.

I just did laundry

Sarah resting on the towels

I'll press them for you!

Something to get your paws on: The heaviest cat breed in the world is known as the Ragdoll. Male Ragdolls can weigh 12 to 20 pounds while females weigh 10 to 15 pounds.

I'm grinding fresh beans

For morning coffee, Hunter

Fears the barista

Something to get your paws on: Beagles have been around for more than 2,000 years. The modern beagle was created from several breeds in Great Britain around 1830. Those breeds included the Talbot hound and the Southern hound.

New denim jacket

For my charming terrier

Now he's modeling

Something to get your paws on: The Harrier is a British hound commonly used for hunting hares by trailing them. Harriers are typically smaller than foxhounds, but bigger than beagles. "Harrier" also refers to a plane in England's Royal Air Force.

Bella loves using

My slippers to stay afloat

As she swims today

Something to get your paws on: The Korat originated in Siam (or modern Thailand). Originally known as the Si Siwat cat, the name changed after King Rama IV was given one. The king was told the cat was from the Korat region of the country. Some people view the cat as a good luck charm.

Nala mad at me

Keeping her from the kitchen

As I mop the floor

Something to get your paws on: The Iditarod is an Alaskan trail sled dog race that starts in Anchorage and ends in Nome. The annual race can take anywhere from 9 to 15 days since blizzard-like conditions are common along the course.

A husband passes,

Bereft, aching with pure grief

Sparky gives me hope

Something to get your paws on: The Aegean cat is the first cat breed developed in Greece. Researchers created the breed in 1990. It is a semi long-haired cat that is quite agile.

Reviewing spreadsheet

My Nessa impedes my work

Blocks screen with front leg

Something to get your paws on: When a cat chases its prey, it's head level. By comparison, dogs tend to bob their heads during a chase.

Charlie won't sit still

But obeys the dog walker

Leaves me struggling

Something to get your paws on: The Tosa Ken is a dog breed originally developed in Japan. They were developed in the nineteenth century from a dog known as the Shikoku Inu, which weighed between 25 and 50 pounds. By comparison, a Tosa may weigh between 125 and 200 pounds.

Woke up with scratches

On both of my hands, Penny

Was busy last night

Something to get your paws on: The word "mutt" most probably came from the term "muttonhead," which typically describes a person who is not very bright. The term originated in the early 20th century and referred to mongrels.

My Nico jumps and

Tries to bite my outstretched hand

To gather a treat

Something to get your paws on: The technical name for a mass found in the gastrointestinal tract is a "bezoar." A "trichobezoar" is more commonly known to cat owners as a "hairball."

Leaving the kennel

Her generous heart aching,

So many to save

Something to get your paws on: When cats go into heat, the four-stage process is known as "estrus." The stages are called: proestrus, estrus, metestrus and anestrus.

Tarun Reddy

Convincing a friend,

To adopt a gray tabby

For pure enjoyment

Something to get your paws on: While many people believe the greyhound is the fastest dog breed, many researchers believe the Sighthound or Whippet is the fastest dog.

Jogger stops running

A flyer on pole mentions

A lost Labrador

Something to get your paws on: Most male cats tend to have more strength in their left paws while female cats have greater strength in their right paws.

Misha gets restless

Climbing on my comfy jeans

Not making progress

Something to get your paws on: Greyhounds, according to researchers, are among the healthiest of dog breeds. One of the more common ailments they may experience is known as "esophageal achalasia" which refers to difficulty swallowing food.

Henry spying my

Yogurt wanting some but it

Has too much sugar

Something to get your paws on: Audiologists have determined that cats make 100 different sounds. By comparison, dogs only have 10 different sounds. Cat sounds are often classified as: meows, purrs, gurgles and beeps.

Henry sees chopsticks

Rolling them forward and back

Such a simple toy

Something to get your paws on: Cats cannot climb down a tree head first. That is because every claw points the same way. As a result, they must back down.

Nessa adores the

Holiday lights turning on

Staring intently

Something to get your paws on: The Papillion is a toy breed of poodles. The word "Papillion" is French for "butterfly." The name fits the breed because of the long and fringed hair on its ears.

Tarun Reddy

Chill won't stop Carter

From enjoying Monday as

He lounges in snow

Something to get your paws on: Rottweilers get their name from the German town of Rottweil.   Roman armies would sometimes leave their dogs in town before heading to war.   In other instances, Roman soldiers would take their Rottweilers with them to help heard cattle over the Alps.

Chester's bad habit

Chewing on the couch cushions

Great dog otherwise

Something to get your paws on: From a biological standpoint, a cat's brain is more similar to a human's brain than that of a dog. Both cats and humans have identical regions that are responsible for emotions.

I rub my belly

Hunter barks and jumps, maybe

He knows I'm pregnant

Something to get your paws on: During the Spanish Inquisition, Pope Innocent VIII felt that cats were evil and ordered the killing of thousands of felines. Unfortunately, the lack of cats in Spain led to a rapid rise in the rat population which increased the spread of the Black Plague.

Chester gets annoyed

When he sees triangle-shaped

Food in his big bowl

Something to get your paws on: The evolution of dogs started about forty million years ago with a weasel-like animal called a Miacis. The Miacis lived in North America and Europe and evolved into the Tomarctus, which evolved into the genus Canis.

Social media

A creative way for pet

Owners to connect

Something to get your paws on: Dogs and cats have three eyelids. The third eyelid is known as a "nictitating membrane" that keeps the eyes moist. This membrane is also known as a haw.

A weird dream last night

My husky driving the car;

I sat in back seat

Something to get your paws on: The name of the first cat in space was Felicette. She had electrodes attached that transmitted neurological information back to Earth. She survived the trip back to home.

Cuddling poodle

As we wait for the vet to

See why her eyes tear

Something to get your paws on: The word "cat" comes from the Latin phrase "Felis catus," which means "domestic cat."

For many owners

The coolest breed of a pet

Is a rescued one

Something to get your paws on: A Brittany is a breed of gun dog used primarily for hunting. While many people believe the Brittany is a spaniel, its characteristics more closely resemble a pointer or a setter. These dogs typically weigh between 30 and 40 pounds.

Cancer survivor

Finds solitude and laughter

With a new beagle

Something to get your paws on: The phrase "raining cats and dogs" most likely originated in 17th century England and had a sad meaning. During heavy rainstorms, homeless animals would drown and float down streets.

Police dog locates

Drugs in a student's locker

In the afternoon

Something to get your paws on: In ancient Egypt, cats held a very special place in families. When a cat died, it was customary for people to shave off their eyebrows as a sign of respect.

My blind pup, Martin

Loves the madness of beach fun

In early July

Something to get your paws on: One of the most popular dogs in Italy is the Neapolitan mastiff. Males are typically between 26 and 30 inches tall and can weigh around 130 to 150 pounds. Females are between 24 and 29 inches tall and weigh 110 to 130 pounds. They usually serve as guard dogs.

I walk carefully

To avoid puddles. Chester

He has damper plans.

Something to get your paws on: A survey released in June 2012 found that 80% of dogs suffer from fears, anxiety and phobias. This study, from British veterinarian Dr. Clare Corridan, involved 1,300 dogs.

Searching for some hay

To make a comfortable bed

For Bella's doghouse

Something to get your paws on: The Singapura is probably the world's smallest pedigreed cat. These felines weigh around four pounds. These cats usually have a brown tinged coat, large eyes and ears. Singapura is the Malay name for Singapore. They are also known as "drain cats" or Kucinta.

Sunrise peering through

The drawn curtains. Hunter barks

As we head outside

Something to get your paws on: Scientists say the earliest cats lived about thirty million years ago. These cats were known as Proailurus, which is Greek for "first cat." The first breed of cat suitable for being a pet probably started appearing around twelve million years ago.

Kendra stands before

Her litter. Eleven pups!

A beaming collie

Something to get your paws on: Dogs have 20 teeth on top and 22 on the bottom.

Splendid, the March sun

Hunter outside staring at

Cars racing by him

Something to get your paws on: The Norwegian Elk hound is the national dog of Norway. It is a Spitz breed of canine and has a very good reputation for hunting large animals such as moose. In Norway, the dogs are known as Norsk Elghund.

Nala is tethered

Staying close to my lawn chair

Preventing mischief

Something to get your paws on: Most cats give birth to a litter ranging between one and nine kittens. In one extreme case, a cat gave birth to 19 kittens but only 15 survived.

Distant barks distract

Me as I struggle with work

Dogs enjoying spring

Something to get your paws on: The Donskoy is a relatively recent breed of feline, having been developed in 1987. Elena Kovaleva, a Russian cat breeder, rescued a cat that was losing its hair because of stress. The cat gave birth to a litter of hairless kittens. Irina Nemikina, also a cat breeder, heard of the hairless kittens and then created a new breed. The cats were originally known as "Don Sphynx," but are now officially known as Donskoy.

Roma on the beach

Follows along soaring kite

At the Outer Banks

Something to get your paws on: Normal body temperature for a dog is around 101 degrees Fahrenheit. When dogs want to retain body heat, they will breathe through their noses rather than their mouths.

Playing some ring toss

Scooter barks when I score; Walks

Away when I don't

Something to get your paws on: Purebred collies are usually between 22 and 26 inches tall. Contrary to popular belief, there is no such thing as a miniature collie. Those dogs are typically Shetland sheepdogs, which is a completely different breed.

Sarah trying to

Climb a sapling without luck,

But great comedy

Something to get your paws on: Kittens have their eyes closed until two weeks after birth. After that, vision typically remains fuzzy until they reach two months of age.

My cat seems British;

She enjoys a spot of tea,

On cloudy mornings

Something to get your paws on: While cats may rub against your leg for affection, they do this for another important reason. Cats use rubbing as a way to mark their territory. A cat's scent glands are located on its face and tail.

Soccer match delayed

After collies run onto

Field after goal scored

Something to get your paws on: Puppies start getting teeth at about two weeks of birth and their complete set of baby teeth will be in use for about 12 weeks. A dog generally has all 42 of its adult teeth by the time it is seven months old.

My thirsty lawn needs

The sprinkler. Carter enjoys

Running through the mist

Something to get your paws on: Not all dogs are capable of swimming. Canines with large chests are less likely to enjoy swimming compared with smaller dogs. A bulldog, because of its build, is extremely ill-suited for swimming.

Shooting some hoops and

Bella peers through the window

I score, she runs off

Something to get your paws on: Kittens start teething between fifteen and seventeen weeks of age. Their adult teeth will generally appear after six months. During the teething process, central incisors are the first teeth to appear.

Casting small shadow

My cat stops running, rests by

Towering oak tree

Something to get your paws on: A 2011 report from the Humane Society found that cats adopted from shelters accounted for 21% of the felines owned by U.S. residents.

Through the clear window,

Observing two dog owners

Restraining their pets

Something to get your paws on: The Black and Tan Coonhound is known primarily for retrieving and following raccoons. These dogs are a cross between bloodhounds and the Virginia black and tan foxhound.

A German shepherd

And owner on sidewalk, I

Cross to other side

Something to get your paws on: Truda Straede, an Australian cat breeder and ecologist, created the Australian Mist cat breed in 1976. She created the feline by using several breeds including Burmese and Abyssinian cats. The Australian Mist is known for its spotted coat.

Getting second cat

To keep Bella company.

Hope they get along

Something to get your paws on: Researchers are not completely sure how a cat purrs. Some scientists believe a series of skin folds deep within the throat are responsible for generating a purring sound. A muscle within the larynx expands and contracts more than 20 times in a second, which might generate the sound.

Two cats but one bowl

Watching them share patiently

I'm impressed by this

Something to get your paws on: If never spayed, a female dog and her offspring could produce 66,000 dogs in six years.

Savannah curled up

On the couch. Green eyes staring.

Such a sweet image.

Something to get your paws on: When Lyndon Johnson was President, he had two beagles in the White House. One was named "Him" while the other was named "Her."

My new eye glasses

Look much better on Bella

Than on my visage

Something to get your paws on: Richard Nixon owned a cocker spaniel named "Checkers." During the 1952 presidential election, rumors circulated that Nixon, who was running for vice president, had an illegal campaign fund. On September 23, Nixon delivered a televised speech to defend his record and said he would not return Checkers, which had been a gift from a campaign supporter.

Kids running about,

Sunny day at the river.

Panda barks, amused

Something to get your paws on: The process by which a cat finds its way home is called psi-traveling. Researchers believe cats use the angle of the sun's rays to find their way home.

My corgi scratches

Behind her ears when she wants

Me to run with her

Something to get your paws on: The Norwegian Lundehund has two unusual traits. It has six toes on each foot and can close its ears. It is a member of the Spitz family.

My morning workout

Amuses Ivy as I'm

Sweating profusely

Something to get your paws on: Unlike other parts of the world, people in Britain believe cats are good luck as long as the feline crosses your path from left to right.

Ivy slides quickly

On my hardwood floor chasing

A new catnip toy

Something to get your paws on: When Teddy Roosevelt was in the White House, he had a Boston bull terrier named "Pete." One day, the French ambassador was visiting and Pete ripped a hole in the ambassador's pants.

My mini-pin loves to

Tap my head so I'll depart

The comfortable bed

Something to get your paws on: Franklin Roosevelt once hired a naval destroyer to pick up his dog, which was in the Aleutian Islands. He spent $15,000 for this effort.

Cute laundry hamper

Shaped like my beagle, Booboo

Brings back memories

Something to get your paws on: In the Italian version of "Cinderella," the fairy god mother is actually a cat. The name of the movie was called "La Gatta Cenerentola," which is Italian for "Cinderella's cat."

Dozens of wrapped gifts

Lined up neatly, family room,

Hunter moving them!

Something to get your paws on: The small tufts of hair in a cat's ear are known as "ear furnishings." The furnishings keep out dirt and direct sounds through the ear canal.

After a hot bath,

Hunter rolls on the carpet,

Hates the shampoo smell

Something to get your paws on: Many people believe Isaac Newton invented the cat door because his feline kept interrupting his work. But two biographers who studied Newton's life said there's no indication that Newton ever owned a cat.

Bella will pretend

To be dead to avoid the

Unpleasant bathtub

Something to get your paws on: A dog's jaws are extremely strong. Researchers have found that a canine's mouth can exert between 150 pounds and 200 pounds of pressure per square inch.

My cocker spaniel

Loves to jump over small walls.

But this worries me

Something to get your paws on: Dogs can be trained to detect epileptic seizures. Some dogs are trained to bark when someone has a seizure while other canines are trained to lie next to a person to prevent them from getting injured.

Using my flashlight,

Against bedroom wall, Nala

Loves the strange shadows

Something to get your paws on: A cat's jaw can move up and down, but not sideways. As a result, they do not like large chunks of food.

At noisy party

Pasha stands on hinds to get

Better view of things

Something to get your paws on: A cat's ability to twist its body and tail so it lands feet first, is known as the "righting reflex." Cats without a tail do not have a righting reflex.

A slamming storm door,

Luke running to figure out,

Source of the strange noise

Something to get your paws on: A study from the American Animal Hospital Association found that 33% of pet owners talk to their dogs on the phone.

Late, hot summer day

Bouncing on a trampoline,

Gives Chester great joy

Something to get your paws on: In the Beatles song "A Day in the Life," Paul McCartney paid tribute to his sheepdog by recording a high-pitched whistle sound on the track.

Stray collie scrounges

For food near primary school,

A note of sadness

Something to get your paws on: In Buddhism, cats have a very important place. Buddhists believe that when a person dies, a person's spirit is temporarily transferred to a feline.

Wanting to keep a

New grey kitten, but I can't

Take it on the plane

Something to get your paws on: A dog's body can produce 13 of the 23 necessary amino acids for a healthy diet. The other 10 amino acids must come from food.

My kitten loves to

Knead my head, stop and cuddle;

Not sure why this is

Something to get your paws on: Most veterinarians believe that dog treats should comprise no more than 10% of a dog's daily intake. Excess treats may contribute to obesity.

Lima keeps sticking

Her butt in my face. Makes me

Turn away quickly

Something to get your paws on: Cats have 32 muscles in each ear. By comparison, a human's ear contains six muscles.

Tarun Reddy

Lima loves to watch

Over my knitting projects.

Thinks game will start soon

Something to get your paws on: Most cats had short hair until about one hundred years ago. Then breeders started developing felines with long hair.

When a cat stands tall,

While pretending to tap dance

It's called "making bread"

Something to get your paws on: The exact origin of the Bearded Collie depends on who you ask. Some historians say the dog's origin dates back to a Polish farmer in 1514 while other researchers say the dog's lineage started around 1944.

Cat wiggles his butt

In quick preparation for

Pouncing on new prey

Something to get your paws on: About 21 percent of dog owners have three or more dogs according to a 2012 survey by the U.S. Humane Society.

When Penny squishes

Her eyes together, I know

She's showing pleasure

Something to get your paws on: To give you an idea of how fine a cat's hair is, it typically has 130,000 hairs per square inch. By comparison, a human has 2,200 hairs per square inch.

My Ivy enjoys

Blanket surfing at sunrise

Which awakens me

Something to get your paws on: It is estimated that France has about 10 million cats and 9 million dogs.

When Charlie rolls his

Chin towards the floor, it's time

For a belly rub

Something to get your paws on: Starting in the late 1890s, it was common for researchers in Antarctica to use dogs as a primary source of transportation. Specifically, huskies from Greenland were the breed of choice. But researchers, worried about an outbreak of distemper, decided that no more dogs should be brought to the continent. On February 22, 1994, the last dogs were removed from the continent.

Stella loves riding

In the car; protects her turf

Like we're still at home

Something to get your paws on: Andrew Lloyd Webber wrote the musical "Cats" based on "Old Possum's Book of Practical Cats," which was written by T.S. Eliot. "Cats" ran on Broadway for eighteen years, making it the second longest running musical of all time.

New laminate floor

Has dog drool in the corners

But I'm so happy!

Something to get your paws on: Italian greyhounds are often called "Iggies." Unlike other greyhounds, Iggies tend to be high-maintenance.

My Chester enjoys

Rolling on the ground, mimics

Capture of fresh prey

Something to get your paws on: The Pomeranian originated from the Spitz breed in Iceland that was used for pulling sleds. They come in a variety of colors, including black, white, red and blue.

Limca rolls on ground,

Maybe she's jealous; stamps out

Scent of intruder

Something to get your paws on: In ancient Rome, mastiffs were fitted with armor and used to attack opposing armies.

Tarun Reddy

Chelsea whimpers in

Her sleep. Maybe she's dreaming

Of chasing that cat

Something to get your paws on: The Egyptians treasured cats so much that smuggling a feline out of the country was a crime. Even so, the Phoenicians smuggled cats out of the country to sell them to wealthy people in Athens, Greece, and other large cities.

I'm driving slowly,

Hunter sees a clown, presses

His nose to window

Something to get your paws on: In some parts of the world, bull terriers are known as "Pig Hounds." This term most likely came from the Afrikaans word "varkhond."

Cat paws friend's shoulder

Buries her head in his chest.

A charming greeting

Something to get your paws on: A Papillion that has dropped ears is known as a "Phalene." The word "Phalene" is French for "moth."

Chester, next to couch,

Pressing a paw, on my foot

Requires a treat

Something to get your paws on: An English proverb states: A cat has nine lives. For three he plays, for three he strays and for the last three he stays.

When my friends visit,

Hunter strikes a funny pose,

Flexing his muscles

Something to get your paws on: Persian cats have three types of faces: show quality, doll face and pet quality. A "show quality" face is extremely flat and gives the impression of a very small nose. A "doll face" has a bigger nose and tends to be very round. A "pet quality" face is similar to a doll face, but the face is not as round.

Lulu takes soda

Bottle outside, rolls it fast,

Glad it won't open

Something to get your paws on: Many dog trainers believe that border collies are the best canines when it comes to obedience.

My Nala enjoys

Rolling on floor, runs away

Playing tag, you're it

Something to get your paws on: The Labrador is the most popular dog breed in the world, according to registration statistics. In the United States, Labradors have been the most popular breed for 22 years.

Sasha moves in close

Without warning, a head butt

Leaving a scent mark

Something to get your paws on: A dog's sense of smell is extremely refined. By smelling even just a few drops of urine, a dog can determine another canine's sex, diet, health and emotional state.

Tomba loves peeking

Inside the wooden toy box,

But leaves toys alone

Something to get your paws on: There are fragments
of paintings of cats in Crete, Greece. Historians believe
these paintings may be 8,000 years old.

Home from food shopping,

Tomba's licking the bags; must

Put them away, fast

Something to get your paws on: Some researchers believe that commercial cat food lacks the necessary enzymes to promote optimal feline health. Many beneficial enzymes are destroyed by high temperatures used during the production cycle.

Tarun Reddy

Silly Sasha likes

To remove water from bowl,

Makes messy footprints

Something to get your paws on: Chihuahuas are born with a soft spot in their skulls similar to human babies. The soft spot closes as the dogs age.

It's Zola's birthday

The dog park, pampered at spa

Happiness abounds

Something to get your paws on: A one-year old dog has the same physical maturity as that of a 15-year old human child.

Snow is almost gone

Yet Patrick finds a snow bank

Starts to dig around

Something to get your paws on: Most cats do not like getting wet. That's because their fur doesn't insulate them against moisture.

Nala hisses and

Runs under the bed. Wonder

If she's feeling ill

Something to get your paws on: Research has shown that city dogs live on average three years longer than those in the country. One reason for this is that people who live in cities have smaller dogs, which have a higher life expectancy.

Ollie observes a

Red Mustang and he starts barking.

That car looks like mine

Something to get your paws on: A coal mining executive purchased a Red Tibetan Mastiff for $1.5 million in 2011. It is believed this is the highest price ever paid for a dog.

Fearless and active,

My min pin has me running

All around the house

Something to get your paws on: Dogs and humans are the only creatures that have prostates.

Tarun Reddy

I'm waking up to

Hairball vomit in the den,

A long day ahead

Something to get your paws on: During the Middle Ages, butchers often used Rottweilers as security to protect money pouches from thieves.

Fumble for my phone.

Sterling senses this. Turns so

I can snap photos

Something to get your paws on: Burmese cats normally have amber or green eyes. As a result of crossbreeding, there are some Burmese cats with blue eyes.

Using some cedar

To make a scratching post for

My lovely Percy

Something to get your paws on: The word "Siamese" is of Thai origin and means "moon diamond."

I bought cat booties

For Chester. Seems to enjoy

Them. Walking quickly

Something to get your paws on: The first official dog sled race in Alaska was known as the "All Alaska Sweepstakes" and was held in 1908. The race started in Nome and ended in Candle, which was 408 miles away.

Cat's white coat, fleck of

Orange, warms me like morning

Sunrise on the beach

Something to get your paws on: Warren Harding was the only President to have a bulldog in the White House. The dog's name was "Oh Boy." When he passed away, the Hardings replaced him with an Airedale Terrier named "Laddie Boy."

Police dog sniffs out

Criminal hiding under

House; keeping us safe

Something to get your paws on: A cat's spine has 30 vertebrae (not including those in the tail). Between the vertebrae is a series of discs made of cartilage. These discs have a fibrous tissue making them both durable and flexible.

A strange snapping noise

Has me confused. My collie

Playing with doorstop

Something to get your paws on: Cats do not process regular milk very well and may suffer stomach ailments. This is because most cats are lactose intolerant. If you want to give your cat milk as a treat, make sure it's free of lactose.

Sterling loves watching

Robins converge at the new

Bird feeder outside

Something to get your paws on: Some dogs may suffer from polydipsia, is the scientific name for "excessive thirst." There are many health conditions, including Cushing's Syndrome, which may lead to excessive thirst. Cushing's Syndrome occurs when the adrenal glands produce an excess of hormones.

Bouncing ping pong ball

Against the wall, has Hunter

Running back and forth

Something to get your paws on: Indoor cats get their tendency for sleeping so much during the day from their outdoor ancestors. Cats in the wild must often find more than a dozen small prey each day for nourishment. Wild cats must replace the energy exerted from short bursts of speed with frequent naps.

It's been many years,

Since my cat passed, yet I still

Feel her next to me

Something to get your paws on: In 2003, Dr. Roger Mugford invented the "wagometer," a device that can interpret a dog's mood based how the canine's tail is wagging.

A dog or cat's love,

Provides everlasting warmth

On the coldest days

Something to get your paws on: The oldest known cat grave was found in Cyprus in 2004. Scientists believe the grave was about 9,500 years old.

ABOUT THE AUTHOR

Tarun Reddy has been a writer, and sometimes a really good writer, since 1993. He earned a bachelor's degree in communications from Duquesne University and a master's degree in corporate communications and public relations from Georgetown University in 2009.

In college, Tarun completed internships at Shearson Lehman and the *Pittsburgh Business Times*. Upon graduation, Tarun worked at the *Galion Inquirer* as a general assignment reporter and then moved on to the *Northwest Arkansas Times*, where he was the business editor. After moving to the Washington, D.C. area, Tarun worked for several newsletters at McGraw Hill and other companies. He focused primarily on federal science and technology policy and budget issues.

Tarun resides in Vienna, Virginia and is active in the community, serving as a volunteer math tutor for students in Fairfax County. He also volunteers at the Smithsonian.

"Paws for Purrfection" is Tarun's second published book of haikus. His first book, "Brew-ku: Where Coffee Intersects with Life," was an Amazon™ best seller and was published in 2012.